The Ten Comm

1. I, the Lord, am your [...] have other gods bes[...]
2. You shall not take the Name of the Lord, your God, in vain.
3. Remember to keep holy the sabbath day.
4. Honor your father and your mother.
5. You shall not kill.
6. You shall not commit adultery.
7. You shall not steal.
8. You shall not bear false witness against your neighbor.
9. You shall not covet your neighbor's wife.
10. You shall not covet anything that belongs to your neighbor. —Ex 20:7-17

Prayer
Before Reading
This Children's Bible

God, Holy Spirit,
I have faith and understanding
through Your helping gifts alone.

Give me light
to understand God's holy Word
and to live by it.

Jesus, You are the Way;
guide me to heaven.

You are the Truth;
teach me to know God
and how to love Him more.

You are the Life;
give me Your grace and eternal life.

Saint Joseph
FIRST
CHILDREN'S BIBLE

POPULAR BIBLE STORIES
FROM THE
OLD AND NEW TESTAMENTS

By
REV. LAWRENCE G. LOVASIK, S.V.D.
Divine Word Missionary

CATHOLIC BOOK PUBLISHING COMPANY
NEW YORK

Presented

to

_____

From

_____

date _____

NIHIL OBSTAT: Garrett Fitzgerald, S.J, S.T.L.
Censor Deputatus

IMPRIMATUR: Joseph T. O'Keefe
Vicar General, Archdiocese of New York

(T-135)

FOREWORD

THIS book has been written for children and presented to the People of God as a means of fulfilling the earnest wishes of the Church—that the treasure of revelation, entrusted to the Church, may more and more fill the hearts of the people. The purpose of this book is to show you how God has loved His people in the Old Testament, and to help you to know and love Jesus Christ still more when you see him living among us in the Gospel.

Moses wrote about the early story of the human race, how God made the world and man, how sin and suffering had come. He showed how the Children of Israel came to be chosen as the special nation of God. He then led them on toward the Promised Land. The rest of the story tells how the Children of Israel served or did not serve God and how God promised a Savior.

The Gospel tells the story of Jesus Christ, the Divine Word Incarnate, God's own Son living among us. Without Him neither salvation nor holiness is possible.

The more you study the divine plan according to the Gospels, the more you see that Jesus Christ is true God and true Man; He is the center of creation and redemption. Through Him every grace is given to us and all glory rendered to His Father. May this book help you to love Him with all your heart as your Savior and your Friend!

FATHER LAWRENCE G. LOVASIK, S.V.D.

CONTENTS

The Old Testament

Contents *(Continued)*

The New Testament

God told Adam to rule the earth.

1. God Creates the World

IN the beginning God made the heavens and the earth out of nothing. He made the light, the air, and the sky. Then He gathered the waters together in one place, and the dry land appeared as well as the hills and mountains.

God commanded the earth to bring forth grass and vegetables and fruit trees. He made the sun, moon, and stars. He also created the fishes and birds, and animals of every kind, and all creeping things.

Then God made human beings. He told them to have children and to grow and to rule the earth. The Bible says that it took God six days to make the world and on the seventh day He rested. Sunday is a day set aside for worshiping God.

Adam and Eve are cast out of the Garden of Paradise.

2. Adam and Eve Sin and God Promises a Redeemer

GOD placed our first parents, Adam and Eve, in a beautiful place known as the Garden of Eden. He asked them not to eat from the Tree of Knowledge.

Adam and Eve were tricked by the devil and disobeyed God. They were cast out of the Garden and lost the gifts God had given them. All people are born with original, or the first sin. They were harmed in mind and will.

God promised to send a Redeemer. He said to the devil: "Because you have done this, you are cursed. There will be war between you and the Woman, and between her Son and you. He will crush your head."

God meant that His own Son, Whom He would send into the world through the Virgin Mary, would crush the head of the devil by His Death and Resurrection. Mary, Mother of God, is the only one who was free from original sin.

3. God Again Promises a Redeemer

AS the human race grew, more and more people disobeyed God and became wicked. But there was a good man called Noah, who loved God. God told him to build an ark and and take his family into it as well as two of every kind of animal. He said that a great flood would soon cover the earth. Noah did as God said.

Then for forty days and forty nights heavy rain fell and flooded the land. Every living thing—birds, beasts, and people—drowned. Finally, the rains stopped. Noah sent out a dove. When it did not return, he knew that the waters no longer covered the earth. So he came out of the ark with his family and all living creatures.

Noah offered a sacrifice of thanksgiving to God. God promised that there would never be another flood. As a sign of His promise God placed a rainbow in the sky. God also gave Noah the hope of a Redeemer to come.

11

4. God Calls a Man to Form His People

GOD began to make the world ready for the coming of Jesus Christ, His Son. He picked out a good man and told him to leave his country and his father's house and go to distant land. That man was Abram.

God said to Abram: "I will make of you a great nation. In you all people will be blessed."

Abram obeyed God. He took his wife Sarai and his belongings and left his home in Haran. They finally arrived at Canaan. This was the promised land. God changed Abram's name to Abraham which means, "father of many peoples," and Sarai's name to Sarah.

Even though Abraham and Sarah were old, God gave them a son, Isaac. This son was to continue God's promise for those who would be born after Abraham.

13

5. God Renews His Promises to Jacob

ISAAC married Rebekah. After twenty years God gave them twin boys named Esau and Jacob. Esau was jealous because his father loved his brother more. In order to save Jacob's life, Rebekah sent him to visit his uncle Laban in Haran.

On the way, Jacob had a dream. He saw a stairway which was so long that it seemed to stand upon the earth and reach to heaven. On the stairway, he saw angels walking up and down. At the top stood the Lord.

God spoke: "I am the Lord, the God of Abraham, and the God of Isaac, your father. The land that you are lying on I shall give to you and your children. In your children shall all the families of the earth be blessed."

When he awoke, Jacob exclaimed: "How holy is this place! This is the very house of God and the gate of heaven." He called it Bethel.

6. God Protects Joseph and His People in Egypt

JACOB had twelve sons and his favorite was Joseph. Out of jealousy, his brothers sold Joseph to some merchants and Joseph ended up in an Egyptian prison.

But God protected Joseph and enabled him to give the correct meaning of a dream of the Egyptian King, called Pharaoh. Joseph told Pharaoh to store up grain during the coming seven years of plenty so that there would be food when a famine came.

Pharaoh placed Joseph over all this work. When the famine came there was no hunger because God had blessed the people in Joseph. Even Joseph's brothers came looking for food. Joseph gave it to them and then revealed that he was their brother.

Jacob and his whole family came to Egypt—seventy people in all. Joseph embraced his father and wept tears of joy. Pharaoh gave the family the land of Goshen, near the Nile River.

7. God Chooses Moses to Lead His People

THE Israelites grew to be a great number of people in Egypt. A Pharaoh made them work hard as slaves. He commanded that every newborn Israelite boy was to be thrown into the river.

One baby boy was placed by his mother in a boat of reeds on the Nile. He was found by Pharaoh's daughter who named him Moses and brought him up as her own son. When he grew up, Moses went to Midian and married one of the daughters of the priest there.

One day Moses saw a bush that was on fire but did not burn up. He heard God's voice telling him to go to Pharaoh to gain freedom for His people. God said: "Tell the children of Israel that I AM [God's Name] sent you to them, the God of their fathers, Abraham, Isaac, and Jacob." Moses obeyed.

8. God's People Celebrate the First Passover

MOSES and his brother Aaron went to Pharaoh and told him what the Lord wanted. Pharaoh would not listen. God punished Pharaoh, but he still refused to let the Israelites leave.

Moses and Aaron said to the people: "Let every family take a lamb and kill it in the evening. Collect the blood of the lamb in a basin, and sprinkle the two door-posts and the top post with the lamb's blood.

"The Lord will pass through the land in the night to kill the Egyptians. When the Lord sees the blood upon the door-posts, He will pass over your house, and will not destroy you. Then roast the lamb and eat it. You must dress yourselves ready for a journey, for you are going to leave Egypt in a great hurry."

The people did as Moses said. This became the First Passover Supper.

9. God Guides His People through the Red Sea

AT midnight, the Angel of the Lord passed through the land and killed all the first-born of the Egyptians. Seeing his own son dead, Pharaoh told Moses to take everything and leave with God's people.

God went before the people in a pillar of cloud to lead them through the wilderness. At night the pillar glowed like fire. God told Moses to march up to the Red Sea.

Pharaoh and his army came after them to put them to death. Moses stretched out his hand over the Red Sea and God sent a strong east wind, which blew all night. The water was moved back and the bottom of the sea was dry.

The Israelites marched until they came to the other shore. When the Egyptians followed, they drowned in a big wave of water.

10. God Reveals His Law to His People

AFTER three months, the Israelites came to the mountain of Sinai, where they stayed almost a year. Moses went up the mountain and talked with God.

God promised the whole nation of Israel that if they would obey Him they would be His special people, and He would be close to them. Then He gave Moses the "Ten Commandments."

1. I, the Lord, am your God. You shall not have other gods besides Me.
2. You shall not take the Name of the Lord, your God, in vain.
3. Remember to keep holy the sabbath day.
4. Honor your father and your mother.
5. You shall not kill.
6. You shall not commit adultery.
7. You shall not steal.
8. You shall not bear false witness against your neighbor.
9. You shall not covet your neighbor's wife.
10. You shall not covet anything that belongs to your neighbor.

11. Jericho Is Conquered by God's People

AFTER the death of Moses, God told Joshua to lead the people into Canaan, for He had given the whole land to them. He also showed him how to conquer the important city of Jericho.

First came thousands of soldiers marching. Then came seven priests with seven trumpets. Four more priests followed, bearing God's Ark on their shoulders. Last of all came thousands of soldiers.

For six days they marched around the city in silence, except for the blowing of their horns. But the seventh time the priests blew a loud blast on their horns, and Joshua cried: "Shout! The Lord has given you the city."

Every man threw up his arms and shouted. The walls fell down with a terrible crash, and the Israelites captured Jericho.

12. God Brings His People into the Promised Land

IT took a long time, but Joshua defeated thirty-one kings and brought the Israelites into the Promised Land. He told the people that God destroyed the nations because of their wickedness.

Although Joshua and the children of Israel had not yet conquered the whole land of Canaan, Joshua began to divide the land. He gave each of the Twelve Tribes a piece, according to the size of the Tribes.

These Tribes were allowed to take along great riches in cattle, silver and gold, brass and iron which they had taken from the conquered peoples.

Joshua told the people not to worship the idols of the people near them. They must worship the God of Abraham, Isaac, and Jacob, Who had been faithful to His promises.

Samson is able to kill a lion with his bare hands.

13. God Gives Samson Great Strength to Help His People

DURING the early period in Canaan, God raised up "Judges" to rule the Israelites and to protect them from the surrounding peoples. One of these Judges was Samson.

God gave Samson great strength to fight against the heathen Philistines. Samson was able to kill a lion with his bare hands, and he continually protected the people.

One day the Philistines captured Samson and cruelly put out his eyes. Then they prepared to offer a sacrifice to their fish-god Dagon. Six thousand people gathered in his temple, eating and drinking. As Samson stumbled in, led by a little boy, the people laughed at him.

Samson reached the pillars that held up the roof and prayed for strength. He pulled with all his might and the pillars came down with a crash. All the people were crushed and Samson died with the Philistines.

Hannah leaves Samuel with Eli to be brought up in the Temple.

14. God Calls Samuel to Lead His People

GOD also raised up "Prophets" to help His people. One of the first Prophets was a man called Samuel.

When Samuel was four years old, his mother Hannah and her husband took him to the Temple to worship the Lord at Shiloh. In gratitude to God for giving her a child in her old age, Hannah left Samuel with Eli to be brought up in the Temple. He helped the old priest.

God often spoke to Samuel, and all Israel knew that God was making him a Prophet. When Samuel was a man, he persuaded the people to give up idols of the Philistines and return to God.

The Philistines then marched against the Israelites. Samuel prayed and offered sacrifice, and the Lord helped the Israelites to obtain a victory.

15. God Chooses Saul as the First King

ONE day, the elders of the people came to Samuel and asked him to give them a king to rule over them, like the other nations. God told him to listen to the people.

In the tribe of Benjamin there was a rich man named Kish who had a son called Saul. God told Samuel to anoint him to be King of His people Israel. Samuel took a bottle of anointing oil and emptied it over Saul's head.

A week later, Samuel sent word to all the tribes of Israel to come together. Samuel said to the people: "See the man whom the Lord has chosen to be your King."

Saul stood there, his head and shoulders above the crowd. The Israelites cried out with joy: "Long live the King!"

16. God Helps David Defeat the Giant Goliath

SAUL did many good things as king, but he began to do evil too. So God told Samuel to anoint a new King. Samuel poured oil over the head of a sixteen-year-old boy called David. From that time on, the Spirit of the Lord came into David's heart.

At that time the Israelites were at war with the Philistines and a giant named Goliath. Every day this man challenged the Israelite soldiers to a fight to see who would win the war. David told King Saul: "I will fight this giant. God will help me to overcome him."

Holding a sling in his hand, he ran toward the giant and slung a stone right at him. The stone sank into Goliath's forehead and he fell face downward to the ground. David pulled out the giant's sword and cut off his head. The Philistines fled in terror.

17. David the King Brings the Ark to Jerusalem

WHEN David became King of all Israel he made Jerusalem the royal city. It was built on a hill and was called the City of David.

David talked with all the important men of the country, asking that they bring the Ark of the Covenant back to Jerusalem. The Levites, the priests, carried the Ark on their shoulders, as Moses had commanded. David and all the people danced and sang as they went along.

The Ark was placed in a specially prepared tent. Sacrifices were offered and David appointed some of the Levites to take care of the Ark.

God loved David and promised, through the Prophet Nathan, that the Messiah would be born of David's family. His Kingdom would last forever.

David dances and sings before the Ark.

18. God Grants Great Wisdom to King Solomon

AS God had promised, David's son Solomon became King after David's death. God was pleased that in a vision Solomon asked for wisdom, instead of riches, or honor, or victory over his enemies, or a long life. So He granted Solomon's request, and the King became famous for his great wisdom.

One day two women were brought before Solomon and each swore that a certain baby was hers. Solomon called for the baby and told one of his soldiers to cut it in two, and give each woman half. The woman who was not the mother quickly said yes. But the mother said no. She would rather give up the baby than kill it.

Solomon now knew who the real mother was and he gave her the baby. He also built a beautiful Temple to the Lord and ruled Israel for forty years in peace and prosperity.

19. The Prophet Elijah Speaks for God

WHILE Solomon's son Rehoboam was King, ten tribes revolted and formed the Kingdom of Israel. The Kingdom was divided into two parts: Israel in the North and Judah in the South. Under King Ahab, the Israelites forgot the Lord and adored false gods. God sent the Prophet Elijah to tell Ahab that he would be punished.

Elijah challenged the people to come up to Mount Carmel with him and the 850 prophets of Baal, and see which God would send fire from heaven. He told the false prophets to call on Baal and he would call on the name of the Lord. The priests of Baal cried out: "O Baal, hear us!" But there was no answer by fire.

When Elijah called on the Lord, the fire of God fell upon the altar. It burned the bullock and the wood. The people dropped to their knees and cried out: "The Lord, He is our God!"

20. God Calls Isaiah to Be a Prophet

GOD sent many Prophets to the King-doms of Israel and Judah. One of the greatest was a nobleman from Jerusalem named Isaiah.

One day, Isaiah had a vision. He saw the Lord sitting on a throne and angels around Him sang: "Holy, holy, holy, Lord God of hosts, all the earth is full of Your glory!" One angel took a live coal and touched the Prophet's lips saying: "Your sins shall be taken away."

Isaiah heard the Lord say: "Whom shall I send?" He said: "Here I am. Send me." And so Isaiah brought God's message to kings and people.

Isaiah foretold the coming of the Mes-siah and His Kingdom, and also that a Child would be born of a Virgin and would be the Savior of the world.

21. The People Are Taken into Exile Because of Their Sins

THE people of the Northern Kingdom were not faithful to God's commandments. Since He is a just as well as a merciful God, He had to punish them.

God allowed the Assyrians to destroy Israel and carry off the people into another land. There they had to suffer much at the hands of their enemies. But God had mercy on the people and sent them Prophets to remind them to do His will and to obtain His help.

The people of the Southern Kingdom were also unfaithful. So God allowed the Babylonians to conquer Jerusalem, set fire to the Temple, and take many of the Israelites into exile. But God continued to send them His Prophets who helped them keep their faith in God and find their way back to Him.

22. Daniel Is Saved in the Lions' Den

AMONG the Jewish captives transported to Babylonia, there was a young man named Daniel who was faithful to the Lord. Darius the King had great respect for Daniel and wanted to make him chief of 120 princes. These princes were jealous and invented a decree that anyone who asked for a favor from any god or man except Darius should be thrown into a den of lions.

When Daniel heard of the decree, he went to his room and knelt in prayer to God as usual. The princes ran to tell the king that Daniel had no respect for him or his decree. The king was sad, but he had to place Daniel in the lions' den. He said: "May the God you serve save you!"

In the morning the king hurried to the den and he found Daniel alive! God had closed the mouths of the lions. Darius told his people to honor the God of Daniel, the God Who saves.

23. Jesus' Birth Is Announced to Mary

THE Angel Gabriel was sent by God to a Virgin betrothed to a man called Joseph. The Angel said to her: "Hail, full of grace, the Lord is with you. Blessed are you among women."

Mary was troubled and wondered about this greeting. The Angel then said: "The Holy Spirit will come upon you."

The Angel continued: "Do not be afraid, Mary, for you have found grace with God. Behold, you shall conceive in your womb and shall bring forth a Son; and you shall call His name Jesus."

After learning that this was to be done by the power of God, Mary said: "I am the servant of the Lord. Let it be done to me as you say."

*The angel Gabriel tells Mary that
she is to be the Mother of God.*

24. Jesus Is Born

THE Roman Emperor Augustus ordered all the people under his rule to be counted. Joseph and Mary left their home in Nazareth and traveled to Bethlehem.

So many people had come to be registered that there was no room for them in the inn. Outside the town, on the hills, they found a cave. Here Jesus was born. Mary wrapped Him in soft clothes and laid Him in a manger.

Nearby, shepherds were watching their sheep. Suddenly an angel appeared and said: "Do not be afraid, for behold, I bring you good news of great joy, for today in the town of Bethlehem a Savior has been born. You will find the infant Jesus lying in a manger."

Other angels appeared. They praised God, saying: "Glory to God in high heaven, peace on earth to those on whom His favor rests."

25. The Three Wise Men Come to Worship Jesus

WHEN Jesus was still a baby, three Wise Men came from a far land to Jerusalem. They had seen a star in the East and had come to adore the newborn King.

Herod, the ruler, feared this new King. He told the Wise Men to find the new King and report to him.

The star went ahead of them until it came over the place where the Child was. They went into the house and saw the Child with His mother Mary. They knelt down and worshiped Him; then they opened their bags and offered Him presents: gold, frankincense, and myrrh.

God warned the Wise Men in a dream not to go back to Herod. So they went back to their country by another road.

26. Jesus Speaks with the Teachers

WHEN Jesus was twelve years old, He went up to Jerusalem with Mary and Joseph. After the feast, His parents started home and discovered that Jesus was not with them. For three days they looked for Him. At last they found Jesus in the Temple, surrounded by learned men, listening to them and asking questions.

His Mother said to Him: "Son, why have You done this to us?" He answered: "Why did you have to look for Me? Didn't you know that I had to be in My Father's house?"

Mary did not understand that Jesus was doing the work of His heavenly Father. He returned obediently to Nazareth. Jesus helped St. Joseph in the carpenter shop, and when St. Joseph died He supported His Mother until the age of thirty.

Jesus speaks with the teachers in the Temple.

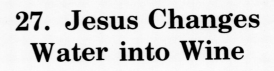

27. Jesus Changes Water into Wine

ONE day Mary went to a marriage feast in Cana. Jesus and His disciples were also there.

Toward the end of the feast Mary saw that there was not enough wine, so she told Jesus. She knew that He would never refuse to do anything she wanted.

Jesus ordered the waiters to fill six big water jars with water and to carry the water to the steward. Only then was it known that Jesus had turned that same water into wine.

This was the first miracle Jesus performed, and His disciples believed in Him.

28. Jesus Heals a Crippled Man

JESUS was in Jerusalem for the Feast of Passover and He went to the Pool of Bethesda. It was crowded with sick people, lying there blind, lame, or disabled. Each person was hoping to be the first to plunge into the Pool when the water moved and so be healed.

Jesus met a man who had been sick for 38 years and asked him: "Do you want to be healed?" The sick man said: "Lord, I do not have anyone to plunge me into the Pool when the water has been stirred up. By the time I get there, someone else has gone in before me."

Jesus said to him: "Stand up! Pick up your mat and walk!" The man was cured at once. He picked up his mat and began to walk.

Later on, Jesus found him in the Temple and told him: "Remember, you have been cured. Give up your sins."

29. Jesus Choose the Twelve Apostles

THE time came when Jesus had to begin His ministry of preaching. He left home and people flocked to Him.

Jesus went up a mountain and remained in prayer all night with His Father. At daybreak He came down and selected twelve men. These were to share His life. They were to be called Apostles.

They were: Simon Peter and Andrew, James and John, Philip and Bartholomew (or Nathaniel), Matthew and Thomas, James and Simon, Jude Thaddeus and Judas (who betrayed Him).

Jesus chose these men to be the foundation of His Kingdom and His Church, because He was to give them the powers of the priesthood: to offer the sacrifice of the Mass, to forgive sins, and to teach in His name. They would take His place on earth and give their powers to other priests.

Jesus chooses twelve men to be His Apostles.

30. Jesus Gives the Sermon on the Mount

ONE day Jesus went up the side of a hill where all could see Him, and He began to teach the large crowd of people who had come to hear Him.

He said that God made us to know, love, and serve Him in this world, so that we can be happy forever with Him in heaven.

To be happy we must be poor in spirit; we must be meek; we must be sorry for our sins; we must be holy; we must be merciful; we must be pure; we must be peaceful, and willing to suffer for God.

Jesus said: "Be glad and happy, because a great reward is kept for you in heaven."

In this sermon Jesus also taught the people to trust in God in prayer, and to forgive their enemies; to seek the kingdom of God and to strive to be holy that they may be children of the heavenly Father.

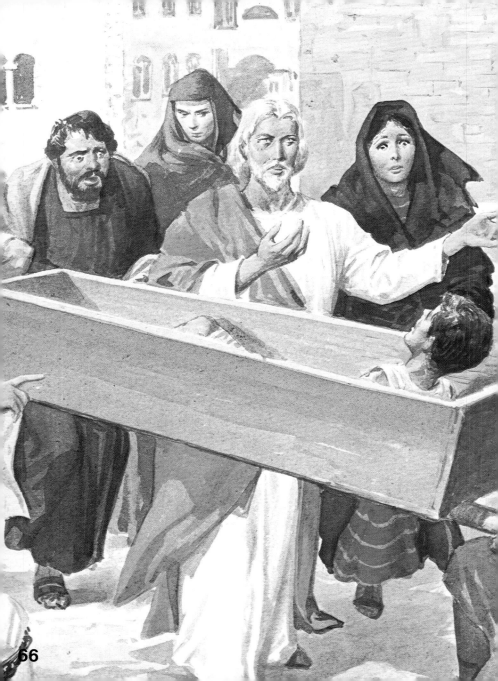

31. Jesus Raises a Widow's Son

WHEN Jesus came to the town of Naim with His disciples, they met a funeral procession. It was the funeral of the only son of a widow.

Seeing the mother's sorrow, Jesus was moved with pity. He told her not to cry. Then He said to the dead young man: "I say to you, arise."

The young man who was dead sat up and began to speak, and Jesus gave him to his mother. Everyone in Naim rejoiced and praised God.

They said: "A great Prophet has risen among us! God has visited His people."

Jesus showed the people that He was true God and Man, because only God can raise a dead person to life. Since He is God, His teaching is true and people must believe.

32. Jesus Raises the Daughter of Jairus

A MAN named Jairus fell down at the feet of Jesus and said: "Master, come to my house at once! My little daughter is dying; but if You will come and lay Your hands upon her, she will live."

While he was yet speaking, someone came to him and said: "Your daughter is dead." But Jesus said to Jairus: "Do not be afraid; only believe, and she will yet be saved to you."

Jesus took with Him three of His disciples, Peter, James, and John, and the father and mother of the child. On the couch was lying the dead body of a girl, twelve years old. Our Lord took her by the hand and spoke to her: "Little girl, rise up!"

And life returned to the little girl. She opened her eyes and sat up.

33. Jesus Feeds Five Thousand People

A GREAT crowd of people listened to Jesus preaching most of the day. They were hungry and there was no place to buy food.

Jesus took into His hands five loaves and two fish which a boy had brought. He blessed them and told His Apostles to give them to the people.

The Apostles passed the bread and fish to everyone, as much as needed. Twelve baskets of food were left.

The people said: "Surely this is the Prophet Who was to come to the world!" They wanted to make Him King, but Jesus went off into the hills by Himself.

After this miracle Jesus promised to give Himself to us as the Bread of Life. He said if we would receive Him in Holy Communion we would live forever. At the Last Supper He gave us the Eucharist.

34. Jesus Shows His Glory

PETER, James, and John climbed a tall mountain with Jesus. There they saw Him as they had never seen Him before. His face shone as the sun. His clothes were white as snow.

Then the three disciples saw Moses and Elijah talking with Jesus. Peter said: "Lord, it is a good thing that we are here."

A voice from heaven said: "This is My beloved Son, listen to Him." Jesus told the Apostles not to fear.

When they climbed down the mountain, Jesus told them not to tell anyone what they had seen until after He had risen from the dead.

Jesus let the three Apostles see some of His Divinity shine through His Body, so that they would remember that He is God even though He would suffer on the Cross.

35. Jesus Blesses Children

JESUS loved little children. One day while He was teaching the people, some mothers were bringing their little children to Him that He might touch them.

The Apostles tried to keep the children away, because Jesus was tired.

But Jesus said: "Let the children come to Me. Do not hinder them. The Kingdom of God belongs to such as these. Unless you change and become like little children you will never enter the Kingdom of Heaven."

And He laid His hands on their heads and blessed them.

Jesus taught the people that they must be humble, obedient, sincere, and free from sin, like children, if they want to come to heaven.

Jesus says: "Let the children come to Me."

36. Jesus Teaches Love for Neighbor

JESUS had just told a Teacher of the Law that the first commandment was love of God and neighbor. Then with a parable (or story) He taught us who is a neighbor.

A certain man went from Jerusalem to Jericho. Robbers took away all his money and left him halfdead.

Three men came along that road: a priest, a Levite, and a Samaritan. The first two men hurried past but the Samaritan stopped. He washed the man's wounds, took him to an inn, and left money there for his care.

Jesus asked the Teacher which of the three men had been a neighbor to the man. The Teacher said: "The man who took care of him." Jesus told him to go and do the same.

37. Jesus Enters Jerusalem in Triumph

JESUS started for Jerusalem once more. On the way the Apostles brought a donkey. They put their cloaks over her back, and Jesus rode on the donkey into Jerusalem.

Great crowds of people went with Jesus. Some threw their cloaks on the road. Some cut branches from the trees and spread them in His path. All the people shouted: "Blessed is He who comes as King in the name of the Lord!"

This made the enemies of Jesus angry, and they decided to kill Him.

This entry into Jerusalem was a sign of Jesus's desire to rule over the souls of all people as King. He rules over our hearts by love.

38. Jesus Gives Us the Eucharist

JESUS knew that He would soon be put to death. So He told the Apostles to meet Him in a certain room for His Last Supper with them.

Jesus took some bread, and when He had said the blessing, He broke it and gave it to the disciples. "Take it and eat," He said, "this is My Body."

Then He took a cup, and when He had given thanks He gave it to them. "Drink, all of you, from this," He said, "for this is My Blood, the Blood of the new Covenant, which is to be poured out for many for the forgiveness of sins. Do this as a remembrance of Me."

Jesus gave His Apostles His greatest Gift—His own Body and Blood under the appearances of bread and wine. He made the Apostles priests and gave them the power to do the same thing in memory of Him.

39. Jesus Is Scourged and Crowned with Thorns

AFTER the Last Supper, Jesus went to the Garden of Gethsemani where He prayed while the disciples slept. He was then arrested and brought to the High Priest, Caiaphas, where He declared that He was the Messiah, the Son of God.

Jesus was led to Pilate, the Roman governor, to be sentenced to death. Pilate found Him innocent but to quiet the shouting crowd he decided to have Jesus scourged.

The soldiers stripped Jesus of His garments and beat Him with rods till His body was covered with blood.

Then they placed a painful crown of thorns on His head and threw over Him a purple robe—the color of kings. Placing a reed in His right hand, they cried out: "Hail, King of the Jews!" They mocked Him, spat upon Him, and struck Him on the head.

40. Jesus Is Condemned to Death

PILATE brought Jesus out to the people with the crown of thorns and the purple robe upon Him.

Pilate said: "Behold the Man! I bring Him out to you that you may know that I find no guilt in Him."

However, when the chief priests and attendants saw Jesus, they cried out: "Crucify Him!"

Pilate wanted to set Jesus free, but the Jews shouted: "If you set Him free you are no friend of Caesar's; anyone who makes himself king is defying Caesar."

Pilate then said: "Here is your King." But the Jews cried out: "Take Him away! Crucify Him!"

Then Pilate washed his hands before the Jews, saying, "I am innocent of the blood of this just Man."

Pilate then gave Jesus into the hands of the soldiers to be crucified.

41. Jesus Dies on the Cross

CARRYING His Cross, Jesus began the painful journey to Calvary outside the city wall. He was aided by Simon of Cyrene and finally arrived at the place of crucifixion. There He was crucified between two evildoers.

Jesus prayed: "Father, forgive them; they do not know what they are doing."

Seeing His Mother there with the disciple whom He loved, Jesus said to His Mother: "Woman, there is your son." And to John He said: "There is your mother." Jesus gave us His Mother as His death-bed gift of love.

Then, with a loud voice, Jesus prayed: "Father, into Your hands I place my spirit." Having said this, He died. The earth shook, rocks split, tombs were opened and the curtain of the Temple was torn in two.

42. Jesus Rises from the Dead

ON three occasions Jesus had told His Apostles that He would rise on the third day after His death.

At dawn on Sunday morning, all at once the earth began to tremble, and in some places great cracks opened in the ground. While the earth quaked, a mighty Angel of the Lord came down from heaven and rolled away the stone and sat upon it. In their terror the watchmen fell to the ground like dead men.

Jesus rose by His own power, a glorious Victor, as His wounds sparkled like jewels. Death and sin were conquered.

The Resurrection of Jesus proves that He is the Son of God and that His teaching is true. It is His greatest miracle.

By His Resurrection Jesus conquered death. We now have the hope of eternal life with God.

Jesus shows Himself to the holy women.

43. Jesus Appears to the Women

EARLY in the morning, Mary Magdalene and some other women carried spices to the tomb to anoint the body of Jesus. They were very much surprised to see the stone rolled back and an Angel standing before them.

The Angel said: "He is not here, for He has risen, as He said He would!"

Later Jesus appeared to them also and said: "Peace! Do not be afraid! Go and carry the news to My brothers that they are to meet Me in Galilee, where they will see Me."

That evening Jesus appeared to His Apostles in the Upper Room. He said: "Peace be with you. Receive the Holy Spirit. Whose sins you shall forgive, they shall be forgiven."

44. Jesus Appears to Thomas

THOMAS, one of the Twelve Apostles, was not present the first time Jesus appeared to His Apostles after the Resurrection. The others told him how they had seen the Lord, but Thomas said: "Unless I see the marks of the nails and put my hand in His wounds, I will not believe."

A week later, Jesus appeared again to the Apostles. He called Thomas and told him to touch His wounds. Thomas said: "My Lord and my God!"

Jesus said: "You became a believer because you saw Me. Blessed are they who have not seen and have believed."

We do not see Jesus in the Mass and Holy Communion, but our faith tells us He is there as our Sacrifice and our Food.

45. Jesus Ascends to Heaven

AFTER 40 days, Jesus led His disciples to a mountain and opened their minds to understand the Scriptures. He said: "It is written that the Messiah had to suffer and to rise again, and that repentance and forgiveness of sins had to be preached to all."

He told them that they were to be witnesses of these things. But they should wait for the coming of the Holy Spirit. As He blessed them He went up to heaven.

46. The Holy Spirit Comes Down on Pentecost

TEN days after the Ascension, the disciples were praying with our Lady in the Upper Room. Suddenly, they heard a sound from heaven like the noise of a great wind. Tongues of fire came upon them and they were filled with the Holy Spirit.

At once, they began to praise God, and to tell all the people of Jerusalem how good God is and how wonderful are all His works!

47. Jesus Left Us His Church

JESUS did not leave us without any means of getting in touch with Him after His return to heaven. He left us His Church, led by St. Peter the first Pope, and by all the other Popes. The Church is our link with Jesus and with the Father in the Holy Spirit.

Jesus is constantly interceding for us in heaven. Through His Church we meet Him while we are on earth and receive His blessings and salvation, so that we may join Him in heaven.

Other Great Books for Children

FIRST MASS BOOK—Ideal Children's Mass Book with all the official Mass prayers. Colored illustrations of the Mass and the Life of Christ. Confession and Communion Prayers.　　Ask for No. 808

The STORY OF JESUS—By Father Lovasik, S.V.D. A large-format book with magnificent full colored pictures for young readers to enjoy and learn about the life of Jesus. Each story is told in simple and direct words.　　Ask for No. 535

CATHOLIC PICTURE BIBLE—By Rev. L. Lovasik, S.V.D. Thrilling, inspiring and educational for all ages. Over 110 Bible stories retold in simple words, and illustrated in full color.　　Ask for No. 435

LIVES OF THE SAINTS—New Revised Edition. Short life of a Saint and prayer for every day of the year. Over 50 illustrations. Ideal for daily meditation and private study.　　Ask for No. 870

PICTURE BOOK OF SAINTS—By Rev. L. Lovasik, S.V.D. Illustrated lives of the Saints in full color. It clearly depicts the lives of over 100 popular Saints in word and picture.　　Ask for No. 235

Saint Joseph CHILDREN'S MISSAL—This new beautiful Children's Missal, illustrated throughout in full color. Includes official Responses by the people. An ideal gift for First Holy Communion.

Ask for No. 806

MY PICTURE PRAYER BOOK—By Father Lovasik, S.V.D. A new and inspiring prayer book for children that gives short prayers for all occasions. Large type. Magnificently illustrated with a full-colored picture on every page that adds to the appropriate prayer.

Ask for No. 134

WHEREVER CATHOLIC BOOKS ARE SOLD

Jesus gives the Beatitudes